Hashcapades
The Art of the Perfect Hash Adventure

Happy Hashcapades!

Clark Haass

Cover and interior design by Anita Jones, Another Jones Graphics
Cover photos by Jackie Donnelly Baisa

ISBN: 978-0-9856380-0-9

Printed in the USA

Contents

Acknowledgments

To my parents, Marj and Herb, for their unwavering support for all my endeavors; to my partner in crime, Lisa, for her love and support.

I'd also like to thank the team that helped me create this book and promote my hash obsession: Sue Mann, Anita Jones, Mary Rarick, Nitya Wakhlu, Karl Lind and Jackie Donnelly Baisa.

Finally, a nod to Julia Moskin whose article, *"The Humble Plate of Hash Has Nobler Ambitions,"* catalyzed me into action!

Introduction

No matter what culture or which cuisine, one universal truth is…leftovers. Move over, death and taxes! Yes, the steak grilled to perfection that graciously yielded to crème brûlée or the baked potato bigger than the state of Idaho is now taking up residence in your fridge. Fear not; this is not the end of the world, although it is most certainly the source of your ever-decreasing food storage wares and possibly malodorous emissions from your fridge.

Fortunately, some frugal yet clever person conceived of what is now the gastronomic equivalent of a Web 2.0 mash-up—hash! More precisely, here's how Merriam-Webster defines *hash:* "to chop into small pieces," with meat and potatoes most often cited in the same sentence. However, the potential ingredients don't stop there. Potatoes and smoked salmon; rice and chicken; corn, mushroom, and crab; and tempeh and yams are all examples of hash, depending on the norms within a country or around the world. The important point is that you have complete control of the reincarnation that is hash.

The adventurous cook should understand that the amount of effort can vary from simply hashing and then frying the ingredients to supplementing ingredients with handy frozen extras like hash potatoes to creating the hash from scratch with fresh, wholesome ingredients hand selected to create a dish worthy of breakfast, lunch, or dinner. Did I mention that dessert hash is a possibility? Think of chopped brownies and whipped cream or chopped nuts and fruit in crème fraiche. Are you getting hungry? What should you do?

Today, right now, is the moment for hash to take its rightful place in your cooking repertoire without shame and most certainly with gusto and panache. And *Hashcapades: The Art of the Perfect Hash Adventure,* is your beginner's guide to unlimited adventures, adulation from family and friends, and reduced carbon footprint from your leftovers. Bon appetit!

The Quick Start Guide

You bought this book or it was given to you and your first thought is: I know what hash is, why do I need a cook book? Well, patience is a virtue and in this case a pictorial overview will let you zero in on methods, meals and dishes. If you're a novice, detailed instructions will guide you from the simple to the sublime. If you're a chef, perhaps you'll glean something from different combos or maybe a hash of hashes...hmmmm...fish or fishes...I won't dwell on grammar. You get the point.

Hash Type	Method
Hash 101	Ingredients have already been previously prepared, i.e. leftovers are a fixin' to be hashed and fried. 15 minutes or less.
Hash Plus	One of the major ingredient pairs is augmenting left-overs, i.e. frozen hashed potatoes added, or smoked salmon from the store. Basic augmentation like adding spices or mixing in cream or garnishing are included. 30-45 minutes tops.
Hash Gourmet	Everything is from scratch or pretty darn close, i.e. not a good choice to make if you're hungover in the morning and want something quick and easy. 45 minutes +

Method Detail: Hash 101

The key to Hash 101 is quick and easy, with no hassles or trips to the store unless it's for coffee. (I find cooking breakfast hash nearly impossible without a decent cup of joe.) The basic process is pictorially represented below. The blocky thingies represent the cubist in you yearning to manifest itself in your cooking. This is a blessing! !

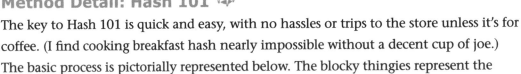

Hashed Protein — Meat, Tempah, Fish, etc.
Hashed Vegetable — Potatoes, Corn, Squash, etc.
Frying Pan — 10 Minutes on Medium High
Hashed 101 — Ole!!!

Hash 101 Recipe Ideas   **Page**

Method Detail: Hash Plus

Hash Plus is really very similar to Hash 101, except you prepare one of the main ingredients from scratch, such as fresh Yukon gold potatoes. In that case, prepare the protein to your liking and set aside. Then simply hash the potatoes in 1/4-inch cubes and fry up for 10 minutes. Add the onion for 5 minutes followed by the previously prepared protein for 5 minutes, then the spices. Done!

Hash 101   Hashed Onion   Herbs and/or Spices   Hash Plus

Leftover Ingredient + Prepare Other Main Ingredient   Yellow or Red (Good for Color)   Dill, Thyme, Cilantro, Chili Powder   Encore!

Hash Plus Recipe Ideas   Page

Method Detail: Hash Gourmet

Hash Gourmet is merely Hash Plus with the addition of other sauces or condiments plus an eye on presentation—stacking, topping off with an egg, etc. Many of these recipes are from the prior evening's meal, which can often be time consuming, so plan wisely and be sure to have a glass of wine ready!

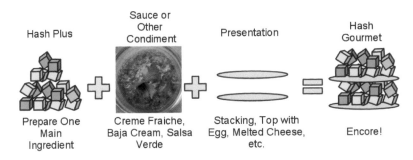

Hash Plus	Sauce or Other Condiment	Presentation	Hash Gourmet
Prepare One Main Ingredient	Creme Fraiche, Baja Cream, Salsa Verde	Stacking, Top with Egg, Melted Cheese, etc.	Encore!

Hash Gourmet Recipe Ideas

Beef & Pork

Corned Beef Hash

Corned Beef Hash

Serves 2 to 4

1 cup leftover potatoes, hashed*

Olive oil
1/4 onion, finely chopped
1 cup leftover corned beef, hashed*

1. Toss the potatoes in a skillet with the oil over medium high heat; sauté for 5 minutes so they are warmed through.
2. Add the onions and cook for 5 minutes.
3. Add the corned beef, warm for about 5 minutes, and serve.

*http://www.epicurious.com/recipes/food/views/
Homemade-Irish-Corned-Beef-and-Vegetables-241623

After a workout, Guinness slakes my thirst and I swear its creamy stoutness pumps me up. But what does this have to do with hash? Ah, it's the Irish connection, the quintessential stout beer anchoring the quintessential hash: corned beef. Nothing like a proper St. Patrick's Day feast followed by corned beef hash the next day or whenever you're recovered and can be trusted with cutlery.

Sweet Corn and Sweet Onion Steak Hash

Sweet Corn and Sweet Onion Steak Hash

Serves 3 to 4

1/4 sweet onion, diced

2 tablespoons butter

1 cup frozen sweet corn

8 ounces leftover cooked steak, diced

1 cup diced button and cremini mushrooms

1/4 teaspoon red pepper flakes

1 tablespoon chopped Italian parsley (reserve some
    for garnish)

1 teaspoon fresh thyme

2 tablespoons cooking sherry

3 slices toasted country white bread, cut into 4–6 strips

1. In a skillet sauté the onion in the butter for 5–10
   minutes.
2. Add the corn and cook for 5 minutes.
3. Add the steak, mushrooms, red pepper flakes,
   parsley, thyme, and sherry.
4. Stir occasionally for 5–10 minutes.
5. To serve, arrange the bread strips in a ring or
   geometric shape on each plate, 4–6 inches across.
6. Spoon 1 serving inside the bread strips and garnish
   with a little parsley, if using.

This recipe has been a long time in the planning stages. I've not passed up the opportunity to demolish an entire steak, especially if it's a flavorful, medium rare cut. Denial is not my strong suit. Finally, I had the chance to make this hash. It won't disappoint you because the steak is married with a well-balanced mélange of sweet onion, sweet corn, mushrooms, and cooking sherry. Don't be afraid to mix up the combo of spices or omit the red pepper flakes. After all, this is your hash!

Sous Vide Beef Rib Hash

Sous Vide Beef Rib Hash

Serves 3 to 4

1/2 teaspoon salt
1/2 teaspoon garlic powder
4 pounds beef short ribs
Red wine
2 Yukon gold potatoes, cut into 1/2-inch cubes
1/4 cup onion
Chipotle Sauce (recipe follows)
1 tablespoon chopped chives

1. Preheat the oven to 350 degrees.
2. Rub the salt and garlic powder on the ribs and brown on all sides in a heavy skillet.
3. Place the ribs in a heavy, ovenproof pot and pour in the wine to cover the ribs.
4. Cover the pot and bake in the oven for 1 1/2 to 2 hours, or until the meat falls off the bones. When cool, hash the meat.
5. Sauté the potatoes in a skillet for 10 minutes.
6. Add the onion and cook for 5 minutes.
7. When the potato is cooked, add the hashed meat and heat until warmed through.
8. Serve with the Chipotle Sauce and garnish with the chives.

My secret obsession is sous vide cooking, a method in which the meat or vegetable is vacuum sealed in a pouch and placed in a temperature-controlled machine filled with water. Times and temperature for cooking vary, but the results are simply stunning—tender, succulent, and flavorful. However, you can make this hash even if you don't have a sous vide machine. The adobo chili sauce is sublime and is likely to result in an extended food coma. Hope your couch is comfortable.

Chipotle Sauce

1/4 cup diced red onion
Olive oil
1 clove garlic
1 chipotle chile from a can, chopped
Pinch cumin
1/4 cup tomato paste
1/2 cup beef demi-glace

1. Cook the onion for 3-4 minutes in a little oil until soft, adding the garlic during the last minute.
2. Add the chile, cumin, tomato paste, and demi-glace.
3. Simmer for 10 minutes and set aside.

Hanger Steak Hash

8

Hanger Steak Hash, Corn, and Yams with Chipotle Cream Sauce

Serves 3 to 4

1/2 pound hanger steak

McCormick's Kansas City Rub

12 cremini mushrooms, cut into 1/2-inch cubes

1 tablespoon butter

1 tablespoon fresh lemon thyme

2 tablespoons cooking sherry

1 garnet yam, cut into 1/2-inch cubes

1 sweet corn cob, kernels cut off, or 1 cup frozen corn

1/4 cup diced red onion

1/3 cup heavy cream

1 teaspoon chipotle chile powder

1. Rub the steak with McCormick's and grill for 6 minutes per side, cool, and hash into 1/2-inch cubes; set aside.
2. Sauté the mushrooms in the butter for 5 minutes.
3. Add the thyme and sherry, cook for 2 minutes, and set aside.
4. In a large skillet, sauté the yam and corn for 10 minutes.
5. Add the onion and cook for 5 minutes.
6. When the yam is cooked, add the steak and mushrooms.
7. Mix the cream and chipotle powder.
8. When the steak is warmed through, add the cream and chile powder mixture.
9. Simmer for 2–3 minutes and serve.

Sometimes, you need to spice things up a bit and there's nothing like the smoky heat of chipotle chiles to boost the flavor profile and give yourself a legitimate excuse to consume a few pints of beer at the same time. Cremini mushrooms sautéed in butter and sherry with lemon thyme provide a nice counterpoint, er, complement, um, makes this hash really nice…

Beef and Cognac Mushroom Hash

Beef and Cognac Mushroom Hash

Serves 3 to 4

4 tablespoons butter, divided

1/4 cup finely diced shallots, divided

1/2 pound cremini mushrooms, thinly sliced

Salt and black pepper

1/2 cup beef broth

1 tablespoon cognac, Madeira or Marsala

1 pound homemade ground beef (40% chuck 60% beef sirloin tip roast, coarse setting)

3 medium Yukon gold potatoes, cut into 1/2-inch cubes

2 tablespoons olive oil

1/3 cup crème fraiche, divided

1 1/2 tablespoons chopped fresh dill, divided

1 teaspoon smoked paprika

1. Melt 3 tablespoon of the butter in a skillet and add half the shallots, sautéing until tender, 2–3 minutes.
2. Add the mushrooms, season with the salt and pepper, and sauté about 12 minutes, until the liquid is almost gone.
3. Add the broth and cognac; simmer until the sauce is thick, 10–12 minutes.
4. Remove the mushrooms and transfer to a bowl, covering with foil to keep moisture in.
5. Brown the ground beef (don't overcook), season with the salt and pepper, and drain any grease.
6. Remove the beef and transfer to a separate bowl, covering with foil to keep moisture in.
7. In the same skillet over medium to medium high heat, sauté the potatoes with the oil for about 20 minutes. Stir every 3 minutes to avoid browning on just one side and season with the salt and pepper.

continued...

They say you can never go back to relive a moment lost in time forever. In my case it was a retro-hashcapade, an attempt to recreate the hamburger hash my mom made to sustain our large family. I remember sitting around a crowded table and eating all the potatoes first before I attacked the undefended hamburger to extend the meal as long as possible! As for the creation of the hash, I vividly remember our big cast iron skillet cooking away with copious amounts of salt, some bacon grease, onions and hamburger, and cubed potatoes from leftover baked potatoes. For this recipe, the potatoes can be cooked in a separate pan while the beef cooks. I cleaned the meat grinder while they cooked!

8. Add the remaining 1 tablespoon of butter and the remaining shallots to the potatoes; mix in for about 3 minutes. Add the mushrooms and beef to warm through.
9. Transfer the hash to a bowl; mix in the crème fraiche and dill, keeping some of each for garnish.
10. Plate the hash, garnish with a bit of the crème fraiche and dill, and sprinkle with the smoked paprika to taste.

Photo by Jackie Donnelly Baisa

Pulled Pork Hash, a.k.a. Hood to Coast Hashcapade

Serves 3 to 4

2 tablespoons butter

1 tablespoon olive oil

2 medium russet potatoes, cut into 1/2-inch cubes

1 medium yellow onion, diced

1/2 red bell pepper, diced

1/2 jalapeño pepper, diced

1 tablespoon Essence from Emeril Lagasse (see
  hashcapade)

1 teaspoon Kosher salt

1 teaspoon freshly ground black pepper

2 green onions, chopped and divided

2 cups cooked pulled pork (store-bought or leftovers)

1 egg for each serving, fried or over easy

1. Melt the butter and add the oil in a large skillet
   over medium to medium high.
2. Add the potatoes and onion; cook for 5 minutes.
3. Mix in the bell pepper, jalapeño, Essence, salt,
   pepper, and 1 chopped green onion; stir
   and adjust the seasoning as needed.
4. Cook until the potatoes are al dente and
   the peppers a little soft.
5. Add the pork until it is warmed through;
   remove to a bowl and cover.
6. To serve, spoon a generous amount of
   hash onto each plate.
7. Top with one egg and a sprinkle of the
   remaining 1 chopped green onion.

Twelve runners, 36 relay legs, 2 vans, 200 miles, and a 6,000-foot drop in elevation: Hood to Coast. What fuel could possibly sustain runners bent on conquering pain and sleep deprivation? From the lofty heights of Mount Hood to the sunny shores of Seaside, Oregon, I proclaim, "This Mother of All Hashcapades!"

*Pulled Pork Hash,
a.k.a. Hood to Coast Hashcapade*

13

Chorizo Zucchini Potato Hash with Avacado Crema and Tomatillo Sauce

Chorizo Zucchini Potato Hash with Avocado Crema and Tomatillo Sauce

Many of the following sections can be done in parallel. For example, start the broiler as the pans heat up, do the chorizo, potato, and tomatillo sections in parallel.

Serves 3 to 4

12 ounces chorizo

1 pound Yukon gold potatoes, cut into 1/2-inch cubes

1 tablespoon olive oil

1/3 cup diced red onion

1 medium zucchini, cut into 1/2-inch cubes

1 teaspoon Kosher salt

Black pepper

3–4 eggs

Tomatillo Sauce (recipe follows)

Avocado Crema (recipe follows)

1. Cook the chorizo in a small skillet for about 7 minutes.
2. Place two paper towels on a plate. With a slotted spoon, remove the chorizo onto the paper towels to drain.
3. In a larger skillet, cook the potatoes in the oil over medium to medium high for about 10 minutes, stirring occasionally.
4. Mix in the onions and sauté for 5 minutes; add the zucchini and cook for about 5 minutes.
5. Reduce the heat to medium low and add the drained chorizo, mixing well and adjusting seasoning.
6. Keep the hash warm while poaching the eggs.

continued...

An explosion of chorizo-based hash is popping up on my @Hashcapades twitter feed. Each tweet taunts me with a delicious picture of culinary perfection or the miraculous hangover/jet lag cure that chorizo hash provides. Well, I can play that game too: Cho-rrrrri-zo Hash—Olé!

Tomatillo Sauce

4 tomatillos, quartered

2 cloves garlic, unpeeled

1 red jalapeño pepper, for garnish

Salt

Sugar

1. Place the tomatillos, garlic, and jalapeño on a rimmed baking sheet and broil on high for 10 minutes or until the tomatillo edges are black and the jalapeño is blistered.
2. Peel the garlic; place in a blender with the tomatillos and mix.
3. Dice the jalapeño and set aside.
4. Add some salt and sugar to balance the garlic; adjust as you desire.

Avocado Crema

1/2 avocado, finely diced

3 tablespoons crème fraiche

2 teaspoons fresh lime juice

Salt and black pepper

1. Mix the avocado, crème fraiche, and lime juice.
2. Add the salt and pepper to taste.

Plating

1/4 cup Cotija cheese

1 tablespoon chopped fresh cilantro

1. Dish out a healthy serving of hash on 3 or 4 plates.
2. Spoon some Tomatillo Sauce and Avocado Crema over the hash; top with a poached egg.
3. Spoon more sauce and crema in little spots over the eggs and garnish with the diced jalapeño, cilantro, and Cotija cheese.

Smoked Brisket Hash

Serves 3 to 4

2 pounds russet potatoes, cut into 1/2-inch cubes

2 tablespoons olive oil

2 teaspoons Kosher salt

1 teaspoon freshly ground pepper

1/4 cup (1/2 stick) real butter

1 large sweet onion, chopped

1 tablespoon Emeril Creole Seasoning

2 pounds diced Podnah's Pit Beef Brisket, smoked
   brisket from any BBQ place, or any BBQ beef

1/4 cup chopped Italian parsley

1/3 cup crème fraiche

1/3 cup Podnah's Pit BBQ Sauce or Stubbs BBQ Sauce

1 cup chopped green onion

Preheat the oven to 400 degrees.

1. Mix the potatoes, oil, salt, and pepper on a rimmed
   baking sheet and place in the oven for 25–30
   minutes or until the potatoes are cooked but not
   mushy. Remove and set aside.

2. Heat a skillet over medium high, add the butter
   then the sweet onions. Cook for 10 minutes,
   stirring frequently.

3. To carmelize, reduce the heat to medium low and
   cook for 15–20 minutes or until the onions start to
   turn golden brown. Remove from the heat.

4. In a large bowl, combine the potatoes, onions,
   creole seasoning, brisket, parsley, crème fraiche,
   BBQ sauce, and green onions.

5. Mix thoroughly and test for seasoning. Add more
   salt, pepper, and BBQ sauce as you wish.

continued...

Now this is not the end. It is not even the beginning of the end. But it is, perhaps, the end of the beginning. And thus, Churchill's quote begins the end of this hashcapade, dedicated to our third annual Turkey Tailgater. His words are especially fitting, juxtaposing our Thanksgiving tradition and the worldwide Occupy movements. Therefore, we semi-solemnly also dub this Occupy CNF—in honor of the dishes that sacrificed themselves for our post-running pleasure at the Portland HQ of Conway Freight. Prepare the day before you want to serve the hash.

6. Transfer to a 13×9-inch baking dish, cover with foil, and store overnight in the fridge.
7. The next day preheat the oven to 350 degrees, bake the hash for 30 minutes, and serve with extra BBQ sauce.

Smoked Brisket Hash

Apple Pork and Romesco Sauce Hash

Serves 2

1 Yukon gold potato, cut into 1/2-inch cubes
Olive oil
2 cups leftover pork and apple roast*
1/2 cup Romesco Sauce**

1. Sauté the potato in the oil for 15 minutes.
2. Chop up the roast, including some bread crumbs
   and sauce.
3. When the potato is cooked, add the roast and heat
   until warmed through.
4. Divide the hash onto two plates and top with the
   Romesco Sauce.

* See http://www.epicurious.com/recipes/food/
views/Maple-Brined-Pork-Roast-with-Apples-Onions-
and-Mustard-Breadcrumbs-355231

** See http://www.epicurious.com/recipes/food/
views/Romesco-Sauce-232504

I always thought romesco sauce was vodka sauce until I actually saw the recipe; remember, my undergrad was in engineering, not culinary arts! This recipe combines leftover apple pork roast with Romesco Sauce. The result is stunning.

Photo by Jackie Donnelly Baisa

Apple Pork and Romanesco Sauce Hash

Chipotle BBQ Flank Steak Texas Hash

Chipotle BBQ Flank Steak Texas Hash

Serves 3 to 4

1 pound Trader Joe's Flat Iron in Chipotle Pepper BBQ
6 cups water
1 cup basmati rice
1 red onion, hashed
Olive oil
1 tablespoon chili powder
1/4 cup Trader Joe's Kansas City BBQ Sauce
1/4 cup tomato sauce

1. Grill the meat for 6-8 minutes per side; let cool and hash. Alternatively, sear in a skillet over medium high for 2 minutes on each side; turn heat to medium and cook to desired level of doneness. Let cool and hash.
2. Bring the water to a boil.
3. Add the rice, keeping the boil going for 8–10 minutes.
4. Drain the rice in a colander and set aside.
5. Sauté the onion in a big frying pan with the oil for about 5 minutes or until tender.
6. Add the meat, chili powder, BBQ sauce, and tomato sauce; simmer for 5 minutes.
7. Add the rice, heat through, and serve.

I've often wondered how hash differs around the country, imagining that the prevailing favorite staples would create new, iconic hashes—Texas, BBQ; Maine, lobster; Louisiana, crawfish. Well, it is true that regions differ, but what's even more interesting is that potatoes aren't the only anchor veggie. Say hello to Dirty Rice. I mean low-down-get-on-your-spurs-we're-goin'-for-a-ride kind of dirty! This creation is really a combination of rice and picadillo, which comes from Spanish and is the equivalent of hash in English.

Grilled Flank Steak Artichoke Hash with Black Olive Tapenade

Grilled Flank Steak Artichoke Hash with Black Olive Tapenade

Serves 3 to 4

1 tablespoon steak rub

3/4 pound skirt steak

2 Yukon gold potatoes, cut into 3/4-inch cubes

1 tablespoon olive oil

1 clove garlic

1 teaspoon fresh thyme

1/2 (15-ounce) can artichokes packed in water

1/2 shallot, chopped

1 tablespoon chopped fresh Italian parsley

1/3 cup arugula per plate

1/3 cup black olive tapenade, divided

1/2 cup crème fraîche

1. Rub the steak with the steak rub and grill on high heat for 4–6 minutes each side or until medium rare; let stand 5 minutes before hashing into 1-inch cubes.
2. Sauté the potatoes, oil, garlic, and thyme in a skillet over medium heat for 20 minutes, stirring occasionally.
3. Chop the artichokes and add to the skillet with the shallots and parsley; cook for 5 minutes.
4. Add the steak and heat until warmed through.
5. Mix tapenade and crème fraîche in a small bowl and set aside.
6. To serve, place a bed of arugula on each plate, place the hash onto the arugula, and top with a generous spoon of the tapenade cream sauce.

You'll notice that many of these hashes are the leftovers from gourmet meals taking an hour or two to prepare. Imagine my surprise and delight when I discovered a hash recipe from none other than Suzanne Goin, chef/ owner of Lucques and an apostle of Alice Waters. This is adapted to simplify its creation. Truly a taste bud extravaganza!

Bacon-Wrapped Ham Loaf Hash with Horseradish Sauce

Bacon-Wrapped Ham Loaf Hash with Horseradish Sauce

Serves 5 to 6

2 Yukon gold potatoes, cut into 1/2-inch cubes

Olive oil

1/3 cup diced red onion

1/4 red bell pepper, diced or sliced

1/3 cup whole milk yogurt

1 tablespoon creamy horseradish sauce

1 slice Baked Ham Loaf, cut into 1/2-inch cubes (recipe
    follows)

1 slice bacon from ham loaf, chopped

1/4 cup chopped fresh parsley

1. Sauté the potatoes in the oil for 15–20 minutes
    until slightly firm but tender enough to eat.
2. Add the onion and bell pepper; cook for 5 minutes.
3. Mix the yogurt and horseradish sauce; set aside.
4. When the vegetables are cooked, add the ham loaf
    and bacon; heat until warmed through.
5. To serve, top with the horseradish mixture and
    garnish with the parsley.

Baked Ham Loaf

1/2 cup honey

1/4 cup plus 2 teaspoons Dijon mustard, divided

3/4 teaspoon black pepper, divided

2 teaspoons vegetable oil

1 medium onion, diced

2 cloves garlic, minced

2 eggs, lightly beaten

1/4 cup minced fresh Italian parsley

1 teaspoon fresh thyme

1/4 teaspoon hot sauce (I use Cholula Hot Sauce)

I have fond memories of our family's dear friend Helen Samp and her amazing ham loaf. On holidays and other special occasions, our family gathered to devour her amazing rolls and taste-defying ham loaf. So, when a co-worker mentioned her ham loaf recipe, I clearly had a line of sight to my next hashcapade.

continued...

1 pinch ground cloves

1 pinch ground allspice

1/2 cup plain yogurt

1 pound ground pork

1 pound ground ham, resembling bread crumbs

2 cups fresh bread crumbs

8–12 slices bacon (8 ounces, not thick slabs)

1. Preheat the oven to 350 degrees and line a rimmed baking sheet with foil. Set aside.
2. For the glaze, mix the honey, 1/4 cup of the mustard, and 1/4 teaspoon of the pepper in a small saucepan over low heat until combined; set aside.
3. Heat a medium skillet to medium; add the oil and onion and cook until softened, about 5 minutes. Add the garlic and cook until fragrant, 30 seconds. Set aside.
4. In a large bowl, mix the eggs, the remaining 2 teaspoons mustard, the remaining 1/2 teaspoon pepper, parsley, thyme, hot sauce, cloves, allspice, and yogurt.
5. Add the ground pork, ground ham, bread crumbs, and reserved onion and garlic; mix until it no longer sticks to the bowl.
6. Turn the mixture onto the prepared baking sheet and shape into a 5×9-inch rounded loaf.
7. Brush the loaf with half the glaze and top with the bacon, overlapping slightly crosswise along the top to cover the surface. With a spatula, tuck the bacon ends underneath the loaf.
8. Bake about 1 hour, until the bacon is crisp and the internal temperature registers 160 degrees.
9. Remove from the oven, increase the temperature to 450 degrees, coat the loaf with the rest of the glaze, and bake until the glaze bubbles and turns golden, 5–10 minutes.
10. Cool at least 20 minutes before using.

(Source: Unknown)

Bacon Hash with Fig Jam and Dijon

Serves 3 to 4

Olive oil
Salt
1 russet potato
1 sweet potato

1. Preheat the oven to 425 degrees.
2. Drizzle the oil over the russet potato and salt liberally.
3. Place both potatoes in a baking dish, cover, and roast for 45–50 minutes.
4. Let cool, then hash into 3/8-inch cubes max.

Note: The bacon can be baked while the potatoes are roasting, but watch carefully so it doesn't burn.

Bacon Bowl

12 strips regular bacon, sliced in half lengthwise, then halved
1 mini-muffin pan

1. If not baking with the potatoes, lower the oven heat to 400 degrees.
2. Using 9 of the leanest slices of bacon, weave a mat similar to the photo shown on page 28.
3. Place the muffin tin upside-down and place the bacon over the tin, molding to its contours.
4. Bake for 25 minutes; broil for about 5 minutes to crisp the bacon further.
5. Remove from the oven and let cool.

They say bacon is the "gateway meat." For me it's now become the takedown meat. To be exact, the Portland Bacon Takedown, spearheaded by Brooklyn's Matt Timms, was in Portland. Matt invited me to participate after his friend referred him to my Hashcapades blog. He hooked me into the takedown with his suggestion: bacon hash. Well, this was just too much fun to pass up!

Bacon Hash with Fig Jam and Dijon

continued...

Caramelized Onions & Bacon

1 tablespoon butter

1 sweet onion (Vidalia or Walla Walla), coarsely chopped

12 ounces thick bacon (I used a Stack Pack of Hempler's Natural Uncured Bacon)

1. Separate the bacon bowls with kitchen shears or use a knife.
2. Put the butter and onions in a skillet over medium high heat.
3. Stir the onions occasionally until slightly translucent, but don't let them burn.
4. Turn the heat to medium low and caramelize for 20–30 minutes, stirring occasionally. Remove from the skillet.
5. Chop the bacon cross-wise into 1/2 inch- or smaller strips.
6. In the same skillet, fry the bacon over medium heat until it is fairly crispy; drain excess fat.

Bringing the Hash Together

2 Italian kale leaves, coarsely chopped

1 teaspoon kosher salt

1 tablespoon olive oil

3–4 tablespoons crème fraiche

2 green onions, sliced cross-wise, divided

1. Return the onion and potatoes to the skillet and add the kale, salt, and oil.
2. Stir and heat through, about 5 minutes.
3. Remove from the heat and transfer to a bowl.
4. Slowly add enough crème fraiche to the bowl, just to help the mixture bind a bit but not be runny.
5. Add some green onion, reserving a bit for garnish

Plating

1/2 teaspoon fig jam (I use Dalmatia)

1/2 teaspoon Country Dijon mustard

Bacon Weave

1. Spread the jam into each bacon bowl bottom and up the sides; repeat with the mustard.
2. Spoon a few spoonfuls of the hash into the bacon bowl.
3. Garnish with some green onion.

Beer-Braised Pork Belly, Sweet Potato, and Chanterelle Hash

Serves 3 to 4

So, a few modifications.

I added a sprig of fresh rosemary in the braising liquid.

For the chanterelles, I sweated them in 2 tablespoons of butter, then added 1/4 cup of cooking sherry and 1 teaspoon of fresh thyme.

Finally, rather than wait for the pork belly to be done, I used 2 tablespoons of bacon fat and cooked them for about 15 minutes before adding the shallots for the final 5 or so minutes.

I also used the pork belly immediately rather than press and refrigerate overnight—I was hungry!

* http://www.bonappetit.com/recipes/2011/09/ sweet-potato-pork-belly-hash

"Psssst! Clark!" Kathy whispered. Before I could respond, she thrust a document into my hands, performed a perfect pirouette, and left my cube. Browsing the two-page black-and-white copy, I could only chuckle as I realized it was a recipe from Bon Appetit* for Sweet Potato Pork Belly Hash. My peeps were feeding my hashcapade obsession!

Beer-Braised Pork Belly, Sweet Potato, and Chanterelle Hash

Potato Hash with Chipotle Carnitas

Potato Hash with Chipotle Carnitas

Serves 3

2–3 cups pulled Chipotle Carnitas*

1/2 cup carnitas broth

2 tablespoons olive oil

3 medium russet potatoes, unpeeled and cut into
    1/2-inch cubes

1/3 cup diced yellow onion

2 cloves garlic, minced

2 tablespoons real butter

1 tablespoon dried parsley

1 teaspoon Kosher salt

1/2 teaspoon freshly ground black pepper

1. Prepare the Chipotle Carnitas; set aside with the broth.
2. Set a skillet over medium heat, wait for it to get hot, add the oil then the potatoes, and cook for 15 minutes. Add the onions and cook for about 5 minutes.
3. When the potatoes and onions are tender, add the garlic, butter, and parsley; stir for about 2 minutes.
4. Add the salt and pepper, taste, and adjust as needed.

Plating

3 fried eggs

1/3 cup Cotija cheese, divided

1/4 cup chopped fresh cilantro, divided

1. Stir the reserved carnitas broth into the reserved carnitas and set aside.

continued...

Yes, I speak Nahuatl, the ancient tongue of the Aztecs. Do you? Well, of course! You see, the word chipotle comes from Nahuatl (as does avocado), and we all deftly pronounce them. As for me, chipotle conjures up a vision of a rustic, spicy, smoky mystery that is simply amazing in almost any dish. So when my son, Alex, suggested we make Chipotle Carnitas, I was all in! Four hours later I was expecting a carnitas baby and plotting the perfect use of the abundant carnitas that remained: Potato Hash with Chipotle Carnitas.

2. Spoon about 1 cup of the potato hash on each
   plate; spread flat.
3. Top with one-third of the carnitas; sprinkle with the cheese and cilantro.
4. Top with 1 egg and sprinkle with more cheese and cilantro.

*http://i.imgur.com/dxwRT.jpg

Photo by Jackie Donnelly Baisa

Poultry

Roast Chicken-Chipotle Nacho Egg Hash

Roast Chicken-Chipotle Nacho Egg Hash

Serves 3 to 4

Leftover Roast Chicken-Chipotle Nachos
   (recipe follows)
Olive oil
4 eggs, whisked
1 roma tomato, diced
1/4 cup shredded Jack cheese
2 tablespoons salsa
2 cilantro sprigs (optional)

1.   Chop the Roast Chicken-Chipotle into quarters.
2.   Heat the mixture in a medium skillet over medium
     high with a splash of the oil for about 5 minutes.
3.   Stir in the eggs, mixing occasionally for about 4
     minutes.
4.   Remove the mixture when the eggs are scrambled
     to your liking.
5.   Spoon onto plates and top with the tomatoes,
     cheese, and salsa.
6.   Garnish with cilantro sprigs, if using.

Roast Chicken-Chipotle Nachos
2 cups rotisserie chicken
1/2 cup chopped onion
1 tablespoon olive oil
1/2 teaspoon cumin seeds
1/2 teaspoon dried oregano
1 or 2 canned chipotle chiles, chopped
2 tablespoons tomato paste
1 tablespoon white wine vinegar
1/2 cup water

continued...

Mmmmmm, New Year's Eve appetizers make a fabulous hash for New Year's Day, reminiscent of migas. My son and I made the appetizers, Roast Chicken-Chipotle Nachos, the night before. On New Year's Day I simply quartered the leftovers, scrambled them into an egg hash, and topped it with tomato, Jack cheese, and salsa. Ole!

1. Shred the breasts and thighs into bite-size pieces.
2. Sauté the onions in the oil until they start to brown, about 5 minutes.
3. Add the cumin and oregano; stir briefly for 30 seconds.
4. Add the chiles, tomato paste, vinegar, and water; bring to a boil, reduce the heat, and simmer for about 5 minutes.
5. Add the chicken and stir until hot.

(adapted from *Sunset Magazine,* January 2002)

Chicken and Four Potato Hash

Serves 1 to 2

Olive oil

4 each Yukon gold, russet, red, and white potatoes

Salt

1 rotisserie chicken breast, skin removed, shredded into bite-size pieces

1 green onion, sliced

1/4 yellow bell pepper, roasted and diced

1/4 red bell pepper, roasted and diced (plus
   1 teaspoon for plating)

1 grilled artichoke heart, chopped (I use Napoleon
   brand)

1/3–1/2 cup salsa verde

2 tablespoons chopped fresh cilantro

Avocado Crema Sauce (recipe follows)

1. Preheat the oven to 425 degrees.
2. In a rimmed baking sheet, drizzle the oil over the potatoes, salt liberally, cover, and roast in the oven for 45–50 minutes.
3. Let cool; hash half of each potato (reserving the rest for another recipe) into 1/2-inch cubes, and fry in some oil in a skillet over medium high for 5 minutes.
4. Add the chicken, onion, bell peppers, artichoke heart, and salsa. Lower the heat to medium and cook until the chicken is warmed through.
5. Remove the hash and transfer to a bowl.
6. Slowly add enough salsa verde into the hash to help the mixture bind and be sticky for plating.
7. Add the cilantro and mix thoroughly.

continued...

You've heard of quattro formaggi ravioli, right? Well, this here is not four cheese but four potatoes and chicken hash, or quattro patate e pollo hash!

Chicken and Four Potato Hash

Avocado Crema Sauce

1/4 avocado, finely diced

3 tablespoons crème fraiche

1 tablespoon fresh lime juice

Salt and freshly ground black pepper

1. Mix the avocado, crème fraiche, and lime juice together.
2. Add the salt and pepper to taste.

Plating

Avocado Crema Sauce

1 teaspoon chopped cilantro

1 teaspoon diced roasted red pepper

One 4-inch-diameter 2-inch-high food ring

1. Spoon the Avocado Crema Sauce on each plate in a circle bigger than the food ring.
2. Place the food ring in the circle and pack the hash into it.
3. Remove the food ring, spoon additional sauce over the hash, and garnish with the cilantro and red pepper.

Chicken Apple Sausage Hash

Serves 3 to 4

4 ounces pancetta, cut into 1/2-inch pieces

1 1/2 pounds russet potatoes, cut into 1/2-inch cubes

2 tablespoons butter

1/2 medium yellow onion, cut into 1/4-inch dice

1 teaspoon Kosher salt

1 teaspoon freshly ground black pepper

12 ounces chicken apple sausage, sliced into 1/4-inch disks

1/2 pound asparagus

1/3 cup crème fraiche (optional)

4 eggs

1 tablespoon chopped fresh tarragon

1 tablespoon chopped fresh Italian parsley

1. Preheat the oven to 375 degrees and have 4 ramekins available.
2. Fry the pancetta in a skillet over medium heat until just crispy. Remove with a slotted spoon and place on a paper towel. Leave the rendered fat in the skillet.
3. Sauté the potatoes in the skillet for 15 minutes; add the butter and onions and cook for 5 minutes or until tender. Season liberally with the salt and pepper.
4. Add the sausage when the potatoes and onion are tender; heat through.
5. Prepare an ice bath and set aside.
6. While the potatoes and onion are cooking, blanch the asparagus in another pan for 4 minutes, remove immediately, and immerse in the ice bath to keep their lovely green color intact.

continued...

Here I was curating tweets for @Hashcapades when my ever-expanding sense of the hash universe went super-nova: Chicken Apple Sausage & Asparagus Hash Burrito. Hash in a burrito? Genius, Full Belly Deli; a huge thanks for inspiring my new favorite hash creation!

7. Cut the asparagus on a slant into 1-inch sections and add to the potatoes, onions, and sausage. Mix in the pancetta and adjust seasonings to taste.

8. To make a creamy, moister hash, stir in the crème fraiche.

9. Transfer the hash to an ovenproof baking pan. Create 4 "wells" in the hash.

10. Crack each egg into each ramekin, then slip each ramekin gently into each well. Garnish with the tarragon and parsley. Place in the oven for 5 minutes or until the eggs are set to your liking.

Chicken Apple Sausage Hash

Chipotle Chicken and Pineapple Potato Hash

Serves 3 to 4

2 Yukon gold potatoes, cut into 1/2-inch cubes
Olive oil
2 chicken breasts from a rotisserie chicken, diced
1 red jalapeño pepper, stemmed, seeded, and diced
1 teaspoon chipotle chili powder
1 cup fresh pineapple, diced
1/4 cup chopped cilantro
1/2 cup queso fresco

1. Sauté the potatoes in the oil for about 15 minutes or until done but still a little firm.
2. Add the chicken, jalapeño, and chile powder, warming the chicken for about 2 minutes.
3. Serve the hash with the pineapple, cilantro, and queso fresco.

Standing at the produce aisle wondering what to make next, I was drawn to the pineapples mounded on a table, begging to luau-fy (is that a verb?) a meal. Skewers with teriyaki chicken and pineapple seemed like a classic pairing except I somehow had heat—chipotle and jalapeño heat—on the brain. Thus was born a delectable hash full of color and rather tasty!

Chipotle Chicken and pineapple Potato Hash

41

Stacked Chicken Hash and Spicy Cream Sauce

Stacked Chicken Hash and Spicy Cream Sauce

Serves 2

1 tablespoon olive oil

1/2 pound rotisserie chicken, hashed

1/2 yellow onion, diced

1 small red bell pepper, diced

1/2 pound Yukon gold potatoes, hashed

Hash Sauce (recipe follows)

2 spinach wraps

Cilantro (optional)

1. In a large skillet, warm the oil over medium heat.
2. Increase the heat to medium high and add the chicken, onion, and bell pepper, stirring as needed for 7–8 minutes. Transfer to a bowl.
3. In the same skillet, cook the potatoes until golden, about 10 minutes. Add more oil if needed.
4. While the potatoes are cooking, prepare the Hash Sauce.
5. Combine the sauce with the potatoes and chicken mixture, stirring frequently for about 5 minutes.
6. To prepare the wraps, using the bottom of a 28-ounce can as a guide, cut 2 circles from each wrap.
7. Place 1 circle on each plate, spoon 2 heaping spoons of hash on top, layer another circle on top, and repeat with the hash.
8. Garnish with the cilantro and Hash Sauce.

Hmmmmm, how to make chicken hash dead sexy for the eyes and belly? Well, you simply stack your hash with cantilevered spinach-wrap rounds using Hash Sauce for culinary glue, top it off with more sauce, and, voila! A meal for Austin Powers or a teeny, wee snack for Fat Bastard. Do you like it? Do you, baby, yeah!

Hash Sauce

1 tablespoon olive oil

1 tablespoon ketchup

1 1/2 teaspoons Country Dijon mustard

1/2 teaspoon chili powder

1 tablespoon chopped fresh cilantro

1 tablespoon water

1. Combine all ingredients in a small bowl.
2. Stir well and set aside.

Chicken Curry Hash

Chicken Curry Hash

Serves 1 to 2

1–2 tablespoons olive oil

1/2 teaspoon cumin seeds

1/2 teaspoon brown mustard seeds

1/2 medium onion, finely diced

1 green and 1 red jalapeño pepper, diced

2 Yukon gold potatoes hashed into 1/2-inch cubes

1/2 teaspoon ground cumin

1/2 teaspoon ground coriander

1/2 teaspoon ground turmeric

1/2 teaspoon salt

1/4 teaspoon cayenne

1/3 cup water

Chicken Curry Mix (recipe follows)

Curry Yogurt (recipe follows)

Garam Masala Yogurt (recipe follows)

1/4 cup chopped fresh cilantro (save some for garnish)

Salt

One 4-inch-diameter 2-inch-high food ring

1. Heat the oil in a skillet over medium high heat; when hot add the cumin and mustard seeds; reduce heat to medium when the seeds start to pop.
2. Add the onions and jalapeños immediately and cook until the onions are tender but not brown.
3. Add the potatoes, cumin, coriander, turmeric, salt, cayenne, and water; cook until the potatoes are tender, about 20 minutes, stirring occasionally.
4. When the potatoes are done, transfer the mixture to a big bowl; add the Chicken Curry Mix and Curry Yogurt and stir.
5. Add the cilantro, combine, and add salt to taste.

Before my hash obsession, I often thought of making ravioli filled with savory Indian dishes— Chicken Curry (Murgh Karee), Butter Chicken (Murgh Makhani), or another favorite, Potatoes with Mustard Seeds (Sookhi Bhaji). Now hash-manic, I kicked it into high gear to combine my love of Indian cuisine with a food ring presentation inspired by a recent stellar hashcapade at Hall Street Grill. Surely Madhur Jaffrey's Sookhi Bhaji could anchor my culinary experiment at Chez Clark!

continued...

Chicken Curry Mix

1/2 rotisserie chicken breast, shredded into bite-size pieces

1 teaspoon curry powder

1 1/2 tablespoons crystallized ginger, chopped

2 tablespoons water

Salt

1. Mix the chicken, curry powder, ginger, and water.
2. Salt to taste.

Curry Yogurt

2 tablespoons plain Greek yogurt

1/2 teaspoon ground turmeric

1 teaspoon curry powder

1. Combine all ingredients in a small ramekin or bowl.

Garam Masala Yogurt

1/3 cup plain Greek yogurt

1 teaspoon garam masala

1. Combine all ingredients and set aside.

Plating

1. Spread half the Garam Masala Yogurt in a circle bigger than the food ring.
2. Center the food ring on the yogurt and pack the hash mixture to the top of the food ring.
3. Remove the food ring, top with more Garam Masala Yogurt, and garnish with the cilantro.

(Sookhi Bahji recipe *from Flavours of India* by Madhur Jaffrey, published by BBC Books. Used by permission of The Random House Group Limited.)

Oaxacan Chicken, Potato, and Chayote in Mole Hash

Serves 2 to 3

Chicken

1 pound chicken breast, with skin

1 head garlic, scored around the center

1/2 yellow onion, roughly chopped

2 teaspoons sea salt or Kosher salt

Note: The following two sections can be done during the boil and simmer steps.

1. Place all the ingredients in a large pot and cover with water by at least 1 inch.

2. Bring to a boil, reduce to simmer, and simmer uncovered for 20–25 minutes. Set aside.

Mole Amarillo—Chiles

6 dried guajillo chiles, halved, seeded, and veins removed

2 cups hot water

1. In a heated pan, char the chiles on both sides over medium high heat so they look leathery but not burnt.

2. Rinse the chiles in cold water; immerse them in a bowl with the hot water.

3. Soak for at least 20 minutes, saving the soaking water for the mole sauce.

Mole Amarillo—Onion, Garlic, Tomatillo, and Spices

5 garlic cloves, unpeeled

1/4 yellow onion, roughly chopped

2 tomatillos, husked, rinsed, and roughly chopped

I channeled a Oaxacan cooking class from Sur la Table to create a flavorful, spicy, and veggie-packed dish. One of Oaxaca's culinary traditions is mole (pronounced MOH-lay), which simply means sauce. Just as the French have multiple types, so do Oaxacans—black, brown, yellow, brick, red, etc. A defining characteristic is the time-consuming preparation—charring ingredients and spices, soaking chiles, blending till silky smooth. I've set the sequencing of this dish to minimize time by doing steps in parallel and reusing boiled stock. I'll try to call out what's going on when.

continued...

2 whole allspice

2 whole cloves

1/2 teaspoon cumin seed

1 1/2 teaspoons dried Mexican oregano

1. In the same heated pan, char the garlic, onions, and tomatillos until blistered and black in some places. Set aside in a separate bowl.
2. In the same pan, briefly smoke the spices; remove as the cumin seeds start to pop or before the oregano is blackened. Set aside in a ramekin.

Potatoes, Chayote, and Beans

1 Yukon gold potato, peeled and cut into 1/2-inch cubes

1 chayote, peeled and cut into 1/2-inch cubes

4 ounces fresh green beans, chopped to 1/2-inch lengths

1. In the same pot used for the chicken, bring the water back to boil. Add the potatoes and chayote. Cook for 10–12 minutes.
2. Add the green beans and cook for 5 minutes. The potatoes and chayote should be tender but not mushy; the beans should be firm, not soft.
3. Remove the vegetables with a slotted spoon, place in a medium bowl, and keep the broth for the mole.

Mole Amarillo Sauce

1 cup chile soaking water

1 tablespoon lard (traditional) or vegetable oil

2 cups vegetable-chicken broth, divided

1/4 cup masa flour

Sea salt (I used Maldon) and freshly ground black pepper

1. Pour the chile soaking water into a blender.
2. Peel the charred garlic and add to the blender with the rest of the charred onion, tomatillos, and spices.
3. Blend on high until smooth; add the chiles and puree until smooth.
4. Heat a heavy pan over medium high heat, add the lard, and pour in the mole sauce from the blender.

continued...

5. Stir often, scraping the bottom of the pan for 8–10 minutes.
6. Pour 1 cup of the vegetable-chicken broth into the blender.
7. Add the masa flour and blend thoroughly.
8. Stir the masa mixture into the mole sauce and add the remaining 1 cup of vegetable-chicken broth.
9. Reduce the heat to medium and cook the mole sauce until it starts to thicken; simmer for about 15 minutes.
10. Season to taste.

Plating

One 4-inch-diameter 2-inch-high food ring
2 tablespoons chopped cilantro, divided
1/4 cup Cotija cheese

1. Slowly add just enough of the finished mole sauce into the bowl of chicken, chayote, and beans to coat and to help the mixture bind and be sticky for plating.
2. Add 1 1/2 tablespoons of the cilantro to the bowl and mix gently.
3. To serve, spoon mole sauce on each plate in a circle bigger than the food ring.
4. Place the food ring in the circle; pack the hash into the food ring and garnish with the remaining 1/2 tablespoon cilantro and the cheese. Remove the food ring.
5. Spoon additional mole sauce over the hash as desired.

Oaxacan Chicken, Potato, and Chayote in Mole Hash

49

50

Fish & Seafood

Clam Hash Patties from Rhode Island

Clam Hash Patties

Serves 3 to 4

1 cup of clams
2 cups mashed potatoes
1 small onion, diced
1 egg
2 tablespoons butter
2 cloves garlic, minced
1/2 cup arugula, chopped

1. Saute the onions for 5 minutes in the butter.
2. Add the minced garlic and clams (drained); stir and cook for another 2 minutes. Transfer to a bowl.
3. Combine with mashed potato, beaten egg, and arugula; season to taste with salt & pepper.
4. Form 3 patties about 4 inches in diameter.
5. Cook 5 minutes a side in pan with oil at medium to medium high until you get a nice brown crust on each side.
6. (Optional) Top with an egg.

(Adapted from: *The Providence and Rhode Island Cookbook: Big Recipes from the Smallest State* - By Linda Beaulieu)

I've mentioned in a previous trivia hashcapade post that each region (or state) in the US has different hash traditions. Whether it's red flannel hash from New England or dirty rice from the South, the prevailing local bounty and cuisine can be transformed into hash. While perusing the Internet the other day for interesting twists, I stumbled across Linda Beaulieu's recipe for her Grandma's Rhode Island hash. Two aspects caught my eye immediately: the use of R.I. clams called "Quahogs" (Lisa thought it was close to the character Queequeg in Moby Dick) and the construction of hash into patties. With that as the backdrop, on to one of the simplest and most inexpensive hashcapades at Chez Clark...

Salmon Fish and Chips Hash

Salmon Fish and Chips Hash

Serves 2

2 to 3 leftover salmon strips, hashed (about 1 cup)
5 or 6 leftover chips, hashed (about 1 cup)

1. Combine and sauté the salmon and chips on medium high for about 5 minutes. Done!

You're at the restaurant enjoying salmon fish and chips, and you're starting to feel full. What to do? Finish it and punish yourself in the gym later or save the leftovers, create a hash the next day, and stay fit and trim? This is a no-brainer, and it certainly doesn't get much simpler than this Hash 101 standout.

Sous Vide Salmon, Potato, and Green Bean Hash

Sous Vide Salmon, Potato, and Green Bean Hash

Serves 3 to 4

1 pound wild salmon, skin removed

1 teaspoon garlic salt

Salt and black pepper

1 tablespoon olive oil

2 Yukon gold potatoes, cut into 1/2-inch cubes

1/2 teaspoon salt

2 tablespoons ghee (clarified butter)

1/3 cup heavy cream

1/4 pound cooked green beans, trimmed and cut into
1-inch pieces

1. Preheat the oven to 350 degrees.
2. Rub the salmon with the garlic salt; sprinkle with the salt and pepper.
3. Place the salmon in a baking dish and bake for 15–20 minutes. When cool, hash the salmon.
4. Place the potatoes in a pan, add enough water to cover by 1 inch, add the salt, and bring to a boil. Reduce the heat and simmer for 10 minutes.
5. Drain the potatoes and mash them together with the ghee and cream.
6. Return the potato mixture to the pan, add the salmon, and heat until warmed through.
7. Add the green beans, heat until warmed through, and serve.

Again the sous vide. I'd probably try sous vide yak spleen if it were possible, but I digress. What do you do when enough potatoes and green bean salad to fill your vegetable drawer are left over? In this case the answer is hash them up with sous vide salmon and eat it cold. This is a very refreshing hash that spares your kitchen from a mess and your house from heat on a July afternoon. These instructions are for the sous vide-less among you.

Baja Halibut Hash with Salsa Verde

Baja Halibut Hash with Salsa Verde

Serves 3 to 4

2 Yukon gold potatoes, diced no bigger than 1/4 inch
Olive oil
1/4 red onion, hashed
1 1/2 cups leftover Halibut Bites, hashed*
1 tablespoon chopped fresh dill, sprigs reserved
2 tablespoons Baja Cream *
2 tablespoons Salsa Verde*
1 tablespoon chopped cilantro

1. Toss the potatoes with the oil in a skillet over medium high heat and sauté for 15 minutes.
2. Add the onions and cook for 5 minutes.
3. Toss in the Halibut Bites and dill just to heat through.
4. Spoon the hash onto plates and top with the Baja Cream and Salsa Verde.
5. Garnish with cilantro and dill sprigs, if using.

* See http://www.epicurious.com/recipes/food/views/Fish-Taco-Platter-233703 for making Halibut Bites, Baja Cream, and Salsa Verde.

Sometimes, it happens— BAM—inspiration! Enjoying a long weekend, my girlfriend and I decided to make baja fish tacos from Bon Appetit (January 2006 but see Web link below), a culinary feat in patience as we waited for pickled onions to cure, battered halibut to be infused with flavors, and beer to be consumed. The next morning we created a hash with the leftover halibut, Baja Cream, and Salsa Verde. The resulting alchemy was nothing short of dazzling!

Crab Corn Cremini Mushroom Hash

Crab Corn Cremini Mushroom Hash

Serves 3 to 4

6 ounces cooked Dungeness or other sweet crab, diced

2 teaspoons fresh thyme

1 teaspoon kosher salt

1/2 teaspoon black pepper

1 ear sweet corn, or 1 cup frozen corn

4 cremini mushrooms, diced

1 tablespoon butter

Salt

1 large Yukon gold potato, cubed about 1/2 inch max

1/4 medium red onion, diced

1 squeeze (about 1 teaspoon) fresh lemon juice

1 1/2 teaspoons dried red pepper flakes

1 dollop crème fraîche

1 sprinkle each lemon and lime zest

1 sprinkle Italian parsley, chopped

1. Combine the crab, thyme, salt, and pepper in a bowl; set aside.
2. If using fresh corn, cook the ear of corn for 8 minutes, remove the kernels from the cob, and set aside.
3. Sauté the mushrooms in the butter for 3–4 minutes, season to taste, and set aside.
4. In the same skillet, sauté the potato over medium high for 5 minutes, stirring often to avoid uneven browning.
5. Reduce the heat to medium and add the onions; cook for 10 minutes, stirring occasionally.
6. Add the crab mixture, corn, and mushrooms to the skillet and heat for 2–3 minutes to warm thoroughly.
7. Plate the hash and garnish with the crème fraîche, zest, and parsley.

Ahhhh, nothing like a little impromptu hash when you're at the market wondering what's for dinner. Well, I created this lusciously decadent hash from the ground up, no safety net, no wires! Cirque du Soleil has nothing on me. You see, it all starts with the taters, the foundation of any good hash, which begs for Yukon gold—good moisture, golden color, and solid texture. But I digress. The real star turned out to be the lemon and lime zest that, combined with the thyme, created a nice counterpoint to the red pepper flakes used with the potatoes for some heat. Don't try this at home unless you are willing to make it again, and again, and again.

Salmon and Bacon-Wrapped Scallop Hash

Salmon and Bacon-Wrapped Scallop Hash

Serves 3 to 4

2 leftover Bacon-Wrapped Scallops and Salmon
  Skewers*
1 Yukon gold potato, cut into 1/2-inch cubes
1 yam, cut into 1/2-inch cubes
Olive oil
1/4 cup diced red onion

1. Hash the scallops and salmon into 1/2-inch cubes
   and set aside.
2. Sauté the potatoes in the oil for 15 minutes.
3. Add the onions and cook for 5 minutes.
4. When the potatoes are cooked, add the scallops
   and salmon; heat until warmed through and serve.

* See http://www.napoleongrills.com/Recipes/recipe_
baconwrapped_scallop.html

I can't tell you how many times I've made the ingredients for this hash. Williams-Sonoma has a lovely grilling cookbook and the salmon and scallop skewers immediately caught my eye and growling stomach. However, it was not until I began to write this cookbook that it dawned on me how fabulous this hash would be. Yukon gold potatoes and yams provide a colorful foundation for this masterpiece.

Smoked Trout Hash with Poached Egg

Smoked Trout Hash with Poached Egg

Serves 3 to 4

2 Yukon gold potatoes, cubed no bigger than 1/4 inch
Olive oil
2 eggs
1/4 onion, finely chopped
6 ounces smoked trout, diced no bigger than 1/4 inch
2 tablespoons crème fraiche
1 tablespoon chopped fresh dill, sprigs reserved

1. Preheat the oven to 200 degrees.
2. Toss the potatoes in a skillet with the oil over medium high heat; sauté for 15 minutes.
3. Meanwhile, poach or fry the eggs and keep them warm in the oven.
4. Add the onions to the potatoes and cook for 5 minutes.
5. Remove from the heat; mix in the trout, crème fraiche, and dill.
6. Spoon the hash onto plates, reserving a little for garnish.
7. Top with the eggs; garnish with a dollop of hash and a sprig of dill.

This is the dish that started my obsession with hash. I dined at Roux in North Portland (now closed) and thought this was the best hash of my life. The smoked trout was moist and exploding with flavor, yet balanced nicely with the potatoes and sticky goodness of the egg. Best of all, the waitress was kind enough to tell me one of the key ingredients, crème fraiche, and I was off and running!

Smoked Salmon Hash with Poached Egg

Smoked Salmon Hash with Poached Egg

Serves 3 to 4

1 medium sweet potato, cubed no bigger than 1/4 inch
1 Yukon gold potato, diced no bigger than 1/4 inch
Olive oil
1/4 onion, finely chopped
2 eggs
6 ounces smoked salmon, diced no bigger than 1/4 inch
1 tablespoon chopped fresh dill, sprigs reserved
2 tablespoons crème fraiche

1. Preheat the oven to 200 degrees.
2. Toss the potatoes in a skillet with the oil over medium high heat; sauté for 15 minutes.
3. Meanwhile, poach the eggs and keep them warm in the oven.
4. Add the onions to the potatoes and cook for 5 minutes
5. Remove from the heat; mix in the salmon, dill, and crème fraiche.
6. Spoon the hash onto plates, reserving a little for garnish.
7. Top the hash with the eggs; garnish with a dollop of hash and a sprig of dill.

One would imagine that near perfection shouldn't be touched, but what's the fun in that? Following on the heels of the joyful discovery of smoked trout hash, I thought, Why not smoked salmon? Why not sweet potatoes or yams, too? After some experimentation, I'm pleased to announce hash nirvana!

68

Vegetarian
& Other

Pizza Hash

Pizza Hash

Serves 2

2 or 3 slices leftover pizza
2 eggs, beaten
1/4 cup diced avocado
1/4 cup diced roma tomatoes

1. Remove the edge crust completely from the pizza slices; remove part of the bottom crust if it is thick. Cut the slices into bite-size pieces.
2. Toss in a skillet over medium high for about 5 minutes.
3. Add the eggs and cook until they are scrambled to your liking.
4. Garnish with the avocado and tomato and serve.

Sharing a pizza over beer with friends is my idea of a casual, low-key evening. While gobbling a combo pizza with enough meat to make a Brazilian steakhouse blush, my friends remarked that it would make great pizza hash. Huh? Come again? They then explained that they trimmed the crust, chopped the pizza, and scrambled it with eggs. Shocked, yet secretly excited about yet another hash in my gastronomic quiver, I tried it the next morning and was delighted with a new taste sensation!

Red Flannel Hash

72

Red Flannel Hash*

* meat may be omitted

Serves 3 to 4

2 tablespoons olive oil

1/2 pound top sirloin, cut into 1/2-inch cubes

3/4 cup chopped red onion

1 teaspoon Kosher salt, divided

3 cloves garlic, minced

Black pepper

1/2 head small red cabbage, shredded or grated

2 medium red beets, grated (about 2 cups)

1/2 cup water

2 tablespoons cider vinegar

1/4 cup crème fraiche

2 tablespoons chopped fresh dill

1. Heat a medium skillet over medium high heat. Add the oil. When it starts to shimmer, add the sirloin and cook for about 4 minutes to medium rare. Remove the meat and set aside.
2. Add the onions, 1/2 teaspoon of the salt, garlic, and a pinch of pepper to the skillet; sauté for about 5 minutes.
3. Add the cabbage, beets, water, vinegar, and the remaining 1/2 teaspoon salt; cook for 8–10 minutes, just until the cabbage starts to wilt and the water almost evaporates.
4. Add the sirloin, juices and all, to heat through. Check the seasoning and adjust if needed.
5. Serve the hash topped with a dollop of the crème fraiche and the dill.

(Adapted from Cooking Light, March 2011)

It all started out innocently enough as I read the upbeat e-mail from my nephew, Erik, suggesting a red flannel hash. For the uninitiated, red flannel gets its name from the bright (I do mean bright) red color bestowed by grated red beets and red cabbage that resembles flannel. See what I mean? Who knew iconic grunge wear tasted divine?

Spring Asparagus Pancetta Hash

Asparagus Pancetta Hash*

* meat may be omitted

Serves 3 to 4

1/2 pound pancetta or bacon, diced
2 Yukon gold potatoes, peeled, hashed into 1/2-in
   cubes
1 small yellow onion, diced

1 tablespoon olive oil
1 teaspoon kosher salt
1/2 pound asparagus

1 green onion, sliced into matchsticks, 3 inches long
1 tablespoon creme fraiche
1 egg

Serving ideas: Fried eggs, dabs of goat cheese and
slivers of green onions

1. Cook pancetta on medium-high until crisp, 6-8
    minutes, remove to paper towel-lined plate.
2. In parallel, liberally salt and oil the asparagus,
    grill asparagus for 8 minutes.
3. In same pan with rendered pancetta oil, cook
    potatoes for 10 minutes on medium.
4. Add onions and cook for 10 more minutes or until
    potatoes are tender.
5. Slice asparagus into 2-inch lengths, add to
    potatoes and then add pancetta, stirring for about
    2 minutes, and serve.
6. (Optional) Top with an egg.

(Adapted from: SmittenKitchen.com)

*I believe good food bloggers
are interconnected by a web
of culinary synergy. You see,
I was checking out blog posts
from Lindsay Strannigan
because I wanted to make her
Black Truffle and Chanterelle
Risotto. Sadly, chanterelles
are already out of season in
Oregon and I wasn't about to
substitute dried mushrooms
when black truffles were in-
volved! But wait, her blog roll
had Smitten Kitchen, which
has recipes by season, and
I happily discovered Deb
Perelman's recipe Spring
Asparagus Pancetta Hash,
which I modified.*

Photo by Jackie Donnelly Baisa

Tempeh and Sweet Potato Curry Hash

Serves 2

2 cups vegetarian pho
1 (8-ounce) package tempeh
2 tablespoons olive oil
2 cups sweet potatoes (about 2 small or 1 big), cut into 1/2-inch cubes
1/2 cup diced shallots
1 teaspoon freshly ground ginger
2 cloves garlic, minced
1 (5.5-ounce) can coconut milk
1 tablespoon curry powder
1 teaspoon salt
1/4 cup freshly chopped cilantro

1. Pour the pho into a small skillet and bring to a slight simmer.
2. Add the tempeh and poach for 10 minutes; remove, pat dry, and cut into 1/2-inch cubes.
3. While the tempeh poaches, heat a large skillet over medium to medium high; add the oil.
4. When the skillet is hot add the sweet potatoes, cooking and stirring occasionally for 10 minutes.
5. Add the shallots, ginger, and garlic; continue to cook for about 5 minutes or until the potatoes are done.
6. Reduce the heat to medium low; add the coconut milk, curry powder, salt, and tempeh, stirring until all coconut clumps are gone, the mixture is well integrated, and the tempeh is warmed through, about 5 minutes.
7. Season to taste and serve with a garnish of cilantro.

Tempeh. Who knew it was so delicious? Well, not this guy until last night, which seems like a minor criminal offense for a foodie! My inspiration came from Katie Lee's tweet proclaiming, "It's a tempeh Tuesday at my house tonight…making a Tempeh Teriyaki Stir-Fry…yummmmm." Indeed. What about a Tempeh Tuesday Hashcapade at Chez Clark?

Tempeh and Sweet Potato Curry Hash

Harrissa, Cucumber, Carrot and Chickpea Hash

Harissa, Lamb, Cucumber, Carrot, and Chickpea Hash*

Serves 1

Roasted Chickpeas

1 (15-ounce) can chickpeas, drained

1 tablespoon olive oil

1/4 red onion, thinly sliced

2 cloves garlic, crushed

1 tablespoon fresh ginger, finely chopped

1. Preheat the oven to 425 degrees.
2. Mix all the ingredients in a small baking dish and roast in the oven for 15 minutes.
3. Remove from the oven, stir, and set aside.

Lamb Loin Chops

1 clove garlic, crushed

1 teaspoon fresh ginger, finely chopped

3 lamb loin chops or other favorite cuts (about 6 ounces net each)

Salt and freshly ground black pepper

1. Rub the garlic and ginger on both sides of the chops; sprinkle the salt and pepper over them.
2. For 1 1/4-inch chops, grill for about 6 minutes on each side for medium rare. Set aside.
3. Alternatively, sear in a skillet over medium high for 2 minutes on each side; turn the heat to medium and cook to your desired level of doneness. Set aside.

Carrot Salad with Harissa, Feta, and Mint (adapted from Smitten Kitchen)

2 carrots, peeled and shredded

It seems only fitting that the equally exotic cuisine of North Africa—Tunisia, Algeria, Morocco—be my next target. And, just as India has curry and Oaxaca has mole, North Africa boasts a signature ingredient, harissa. Put another way, harissa is to North Africa as salsa is to Mexico. Its pepper, garlic, coriander, chili powder, and other spices amp up any dish considerably. But before you go ga-ga over the harissa, pre-heat the oven to 425 degrees and get the grill going. You will have leftover carrot salad and chickpeas; combine for a great salad snack!

* omit the meat or, double the recipe for a vegetarian feast without lamb!

continued...

1 clove garlic, crushed

1/2 teaspoon ground cumin

1 teaspoon harissa (Whole Foods is my source)

1 teaspoon sugar

Juice from 1/2 small to medium lemon

1 tablespoon chopped fresh mint

1/3 cup feta cheese

1. Mix all the ingredients in a bowl.
2. Check for taste; if too acidic, add more sugar; if not enough heat, add more harissa. Set aside.

Cucumber & Yogurt

1/2 cup 1/4-inch-dice English cucumber

1 tablespoon Greek yogurt

1. Mix the cucumber and yogurt in a small ramekin and set aside.

Plating

2 tablespoons Greek yogurt

1 teaspoon harissa, plus additional

1–2 small mint leaves, minced and divided

One 4-inch-diameter 2-inch-high food ring

1. Mix the yogurt, 1 teaspoon of the harissa, and 1 minced mint leaf and spoon almost all on the plate in a circle bigger than the food ring.
2. Place the food ring in the circle. Carefully pack one layer of chickpeas into the food ring, then an equal layer of carrot salad, then an equal layer of cucumber mixture. Remove the food ring.
3. Slice the lamb into 1-inch by 1 1/2-inch rectangles and overlap in a circle, filling the middle with the rest of the lamb.
4. Spoon the rest of the yogurt-harissa sauce over the lamb, top with a scant teaspoon of the harissa, and garnish with the remaining minced mint leaf.

Thai Yellow Curry Veggie Hash

Serves 1

1/2 butternut squash, peeled, seeded, and cut into 1/2-inch cubes

1 sweet potato, peeled and cut into 1/2-inch cubes

1 tablespoon olive oil, plus additional

Salt and freshly ground black pepper

2 cloves garlic, crushed

2 shallots, minced

1 tablespoon plus 1 1/2 teaspoons Thai yellow curry paste, divided

1 cup chicken stock (the original called for vegetable stock)

2 kaffir lime leaves, torn

1 tablespoon finely chopped fresh galangal

1/2 cup coconut milk, reserve top cream

1 1/2 teaspoons soy sauce

1 tablespoon Thai fish sauce

1/2 red bell pepper, finely chopped

1/2 jalapeño pepper, finely diced (set aside a scant teaspoon for garnish)

5 shitake mushrooms, cut into 1/2-inch cubes

1. Preheat the oven to 375 degrees.
2. Place the squash and potato on a rimmed baking sheet. Drizzle with the oil and add the salt and pepper.
3. Roast for 20 minutes or until al dente. Set aside.
4. Heat some oil in a wok over medium, add the garlic and shallots, and stir until soft to avoid burning them.
5. Add the 1 tablespoon of the curry paste and mix in until it foams.

continued...

A friend of mine (we'll call him Jeff) quietly confessed his secret. "I dabble in Thai food," he practically whispered. Jeff must have known he could confide in me. After all, he had reviewed my Chicken Curry & Potatoes with Mustard Seed Hash. So, I quickly reciprocated and confessed, "I'm, uh, thinking of doing a Thai hash." With a knowing smile, he gave me the thumbs up and thus was born my Thai hashcapade.* Two days later I made this dish into a yummy soup: busting out my Cuisinart, I pureed it, adding some more chicken stock and cream until I liked the consistency. Talk about a flavor bomb in your mouth! You can find galangal at Asian markets. It looks like a woody, thick root. Before you start your journey, sharpen your knife.

6. Add the stock, lime leaves, and galangal; bring to a boil.

7. Reduce the heat and simmer gently for about 15 minutes.

8. Add the coconut milk, soy sauce, fish sauce, bell pepper, jalapeño, and mushrooms; let simmer for 5 minutes.

9. Remove the lime leaves and discard.

10. Gently fold in the squash and sweet potatoes.

11. Remove from the heat and let the squash and potato absorb the curry for 5 minutes.

Plating

4 tablespoons top cream from the coconut milk

One 4-inch-diameter 2-inch-high food ring.

1 tablespoon fresh cilantro, chopped

1. Mix the coconut cream and the remaining 1 1/2 teaspoons of the curry paste; spoon almost all on the plate in a circle bigger than the food ring.

2. Place the food ring in the circle. Using a slotted spoon, carefully pack the hash into the ring.

3. Spoon the rest of the coconut-curry sauce on top of the hash and top with a scant spoon of the hash. Remove the ring.

4. Garnish the plate and the hash with the cilantro and remaining 1 teaspoon of jalapeño.

* Adapted from *The Ultimate Thai and Asian Cookbook* by Deh-Ta Hsiung, Becky Johnson, and Sallie Morris.

Thai Yellow Curry Veggie Hash

Hash Trivia

Oldest Hash Recipe: A college student in Portugal discovered a recipe dating back to the 15th century for Picadinho de Carne de Vaca, or Beef Hash. Can you imagine Portuguese ships sailing to Brazil laden with picadinho? Somehow, I know it's related to Carnival, which is why *Carne* is in its name, obviously!

Regional Differences in the US: Southeast tends to like crab, Southwest tends to like rice, everywhere else seems to favor potatoes and just about any meat. Maine is unique in that it likes lobster and it's pronounced funny, like a cross between Bostonians pronouncing "Hah-vahd" and Simon Cowell saying "Dreadful." See what I mean?

Hash Around the World: In Sweden hash is called *pytt i panna* and consists of potatoes, bacon or pork or ham, and onion and is served with eggs and pickled beets. In Latin America it's called *picadillo* and contains rice, beef, and peppers and is served with eggs or tortillas. In North America and the British Isles, hash is usually corned beef, potatoes, and onion, with regional differences in the US just mentioned. It should be intuitively obvious that the ubiquity of hash means its ascendancy to prominence in your cooking repertoire is preordained and is truly a result of globalization that started just after the last dinosaur disappeared but before gun powder was invented.

Amount of Corned Beef Hash Produced by Hormel per Year: five bazillion cans that, if stretched end to end, would circle the earth enough times to constitute a red hash bracelet visible from that former planet known as Pluto.

Google Results with "Hash" in the Results: 93,600,000 (as of May 30, 2012). Interestingly enough, hash as used in security yields ≈ 67,600,000 hits; hash food yields ≈ 57,900,000; hash drug yields ≈ 9,010,000; hash running yields ≈ 39,100,000 and hash keyboard yields ≈ 15,500,000. I'm from Oregon, so here's a shout out to the Oregon Hash House Harriers! And to security geeks, eat more hash!

Hashing the Sport: Sort of a secret society like the Freemasons meets fraternity-sorority row for runners, hashers describe themselves as drinkers with a running problem. Groups throughout the US set up hashes where "rabbits" hide booze along a running path and "chasers" find them, drink them, and engage in generally unruly and bawdy behavior. Hashers like hash and beer and running, and their nicknames derive from their bawdy behavior or quintessential character traits.

Hashing in Security: Security technology includes lots of important-sounding words like *encryption, authentication, identification, repudiation,* and *nonces.* It turns out that hashing in security parlance refers to a one-way scrambling function (hash) that renders whatever it transforms—data, passwords, keys—into meaningless garble that cannot be figured out by reverse engineering or other mathematical contrivances. This does not mean that the hash you make is meaningless garble, nor is it secure, but it is truly delicious and easy to make, naturally!

Hash Tools: Sharp knives and an innate ability to tell the difference between a 1/4-inch dice and 1/2-inch cubes, duh! If in doubt, have a caliper, ruler, or micrometer handy! A particularly stellar mandoline with the ability to dice is the crème de la crème—made by de Buyer.

Hash Tags: A recent convert to twitter, hash tags are defined by twitter: "The # symbol, called a hashtag, is used to mark keywords or topics in a Tweet. It was created organically by Twitter users as a way to categorize messages." Please use the #hashcapade hashtag whenever you tweet about hash!

Hash Key: If you're like I am, the sound of a female operator with a British accent suggesting that you "please press the hash or square key" is fabulous. It makes me secretly yearn to put that voice on my iPod or wistfully search on Facebook for the Bridget Hash Key. At least I think that's her name.

Index

Recipe names have initial capital letters, such as Sweet Corn and Sweet Onion Steak Hash.

About the Author

Clark was born and raised in Wyoming, but fell in love with the Pacific Northwest after a job interview in Seattle. Eventually, Portland beckoned and his hash obsession began over brunch at Roux. Their Smoked Trout Hash inspired him to not only recreate the recipe at home but to set the goal to write a book on hash!

When Clark's not dreaming up new hash recipes or expanding his web site, hashcapades.com, he trains for half and full marathons, dabbles in foreign languages and works for a high tech company.

CPSIA information can be obtained
at www.ICGtesting.com
Printed in the USA
LVIW022306300712

292100LV00001B